The Lust of Unsentimental Waters

Also by Rosa Alcalá

Undocumentaries

ROSA ALCALÁ

The Lust of
Unsentimental Waters

Shearsman Books

First published in the United Kingdom in 2012 by
Shearsman Books
50 Westons Hill Drive
Emersons Green
BRISTOL
BS16 7DF

Shearsman Books Ltd Registered Office
30–31 St. James Place, Mangotsfield, Bristol BS16 9JB
(this address not for correspondence)

www.shearsman.com

ISBN 978-1-84861-233-4
First Edition

Cover: Detail of 'Downpatrick Drawing', 2011,
by Sam Reveles. Copyright © Sam Reveles.

Contents

Everything hung on the point of being lost.
—William Carlos Williams,
from *In the American Grain*

The Thing
after Steiner

The thing becomes the thing
because of some speaking habit:
a moment of evolution
that coincides with the digging
of holes and proper burials
When we see who we are to each other
we are social,
but what we see, primitive
Monkeys cannot lie because they can't
imagine the not-occurred,
or more so, the not-witnessed
We name
the body of designations:
we arrive at each other
and claim discovery
The root of my language is said
a forgery when another's house
is built bigger
and in proximity
The problem with chasing invention
is the wheel is its own perfect critic
To be the small dog tethered to the wagon
of some frontier
can only mean exhaustion

The Sixth Avenue Go-Go Lounge

breaks
      down
           the language
              of sentiment

and the girl who
speaks
a fluent you
rubs
a little sense
into your lap

four bucks later
you think you've
made some progress —

subjectivity
finally *means* something

Outside
El Bombero wears a paper thin nightgown
once belonging to his wife

and tries to kill Paulie
with an axe handle

Can't blame
everything on
paint fumes
you little fuck

You can't get up for this sort of thing *every* time

And cut rate
like blow jobs
behind
Union Dye
&
Frost Kwik
the Sixth Avenue Go-Go Lounge
is not
post industrial
post colonial
post modern

it's no sadder
than most things

it's not a text
to be *read*

(Hey

No European Sports——
READ
THE
SIGN.)

perhaps
dancer to drinker
ratio
suggests

the inflated
economy
of migration

or memory

You cheap bastard

Paulie, half-
blind
and
a smashed thumb,
says

I'll can make you that
But it won't taste
like you remember

The Sixth Avenue Go-Go Lounge
making no apologies
for your future
problems,

Package Goods.
Open Christmas Day.

Me(tro)polis

So go my tongue
a robot atop
the shoulders

of fury, making men
proud to drown
their own

sons. One lid
fluttering and one
hand digging

the waist
of unreflective mean-
ness.

Because party
fervor rides
on a little

infiltration.
A bit of dis-
guise.

Rita Hayworth: Double Agent

In the follicles sits a dangerously coiled
and coarse nature, from which the genus

springs. So the body's genius
zapped with a year's worth

of electrolysis. She becomes
a G.I.'s dream by moving the border

that frames the face, by deflowering the name
and firing the island extra

who made the dance number
a risk. Still, after ions have cooled,

they invent helpless swine
to be rendered ("Good evening, Mr. Farrell,

you're looking very beautiful.")
at the spit. Or place her

at the ticket booth of a Chinese theatre,
speaking perfect Mandarin. So

much of her choreographed
or dubbed, winking at you

through a ruffled excess. But what's more natural
to a bilingual girl from Brooklyn

than to mouth her country's script? Or insinuate
herself into its defenses?

She throws her head back, and on a long
black glove slowly tugs: "Mame did a dance

called the kichee-coo. That's the thing
that slew McGrew." And though

it's Gilda we want to bed, we catch a glimpse
of something familiar from behind a curtain

of hair. It's Margarita Cansino as the song
ends and the striptease continues. We volunteer

to lend a hand when she confesses, "I'm not
very good at zippers."

Inflection

There is a terrible wind
that shifts the tender insides
of your name,
when spoken
by your lover
who proud
of his practiced trill
extends it
beyond natural borders.

And the dust that
confuses countries
is in your eyes, and you
blink, and you blink,
and you blink.

The Poetics of Silence
after E. Glissant

as a certain husbandry
of self-interest
or as an effacement
of the account

Something in
transition, a *forced*
poetics or necessarily
a *natural* one

As a starting point
or as an end

The mouth holds
all its weight
like hands:
the record of such limitations
the abeyance of song

This elision
or this gathering

A waiting room
where the body
is produced
as a remediable thing,
or in ashes
as a reducible thing.

The Translator's Blues

All this talk about invisibility's
making me thirsty

ships, ships
everywhere

and not a drop—
me thinks

it
strange:

nobody
here

but us
history

Dear Atopia of Bliss,

Reading again, Berryman and other bad endings.
I am a slow reader, to be sure. I've nothing to report:
O'Hara is alive. Benjamin. Why make it
to a French border when downtown
it's all dicks and fists
and Bunny's still at Harvard?

"I should eagerly like to know anything,"
Kenneth. I open you as corrective,
and Daniel is still four years old, and
still the Boss of God. Oh say it again—
Are you a poet like my Daddy?
A vitalist fiction like textual genealogies?

Safe Distance

What we know
about ourselves
is
split
into distances

the body
is part history

sex gives news

When all
museums
have been looted

will an empire
of pawned goods

conquer?

No love
is safe

from this lack
of imagination

We send ourselves off
to work out
patterns

of grammar or war

and translation
as the final instance
of mishearing

sends the
sensitive word away

to seek kindness
in strangers

This poem acts
as if the world
exists

so I ignore it

and it becomes
a terror

to converse with.

How Language Spanks Us

So far, a country that splits itself with laughter at the seams
seems impossible—
it's enough euphoria is textually
incapacitated, everybody turns inward
so that our language folds,
or each person constituting a fascist seamlessness
known as couple culture
creases his answers into precise peaks
like a paper puppet wrapped around a pubescent hand
—a better game than Wittgenstein's in learning how
we might know which husband/car/house will do in what
context—
The promise of pleasure gets us out of the house of our own
thinking, but its praxis or its very pinnacle returns us here,
sometimes with ill-suited aims that are the consequence
of those tight jeans every misreading of O'Hara
leads us to. And despite the pitfalls of
"discourse," bodies against freshly washed streets
sound like new words slapping
some sense against our proverbial asses.

Census

O love,
district us
blind
into regions
of a bastard
science

Our talk
undocumented:
or, who
could
transcribe such
loss?

O love,
erect graphs
of mutant
nations
press bodies
and names
into
the front
seat
of a speeding
category—

Refrain

Today I designed
a noose, and turned
up a song.

*

Postcolonial Watercolor

It could be a country
sleeping between us,

a fen of violets or a fairway
of bay water. A place no one rents, perhaps

a tribe of imperfect relatives
fusing with the sea.

Patria

for my father, José Alcalá García

The salute
of this poem
rides open

to a shotgun—
I carry grief
blatant

as propaganda.
My father's name
lifts

the hammer
bucket
brick

to eye
level
& makes everyone

a bit uneasy
for what's
to come:

a parched code
a cracked
body

's final test.
It's a Dallas
of suspicion

a ramshackle
conspiracy
of origins

that hides
a mother
so central

to the narrative
and fuses
time & again

melancholy to elegy
to bring the madre
patria back

to civil war.
This ditty
like Annabelle Lee

holds the beat
every foreigner
can tap his foot to.

But whose feet
will be put
to the fire

for a democratic state?
When lost
in the sway

of our sorrow?
The flag
of our own names?

Andalusia. Or, a Short History of Dying

El Medina Azahara:

A congregation
of gravediggers

The terminal bar

a Heaven

or a way

A long long shot
of brandy

A bus called in

Córdoba's elite
assimilate a misery

and sing poor, too

Texts on horse medicine
and a girl on a Vespa

cross the Roman Bridge

San Rafael's lit feet
bless this helmet's soul

A marriage at dusk
An adolescent forehead
A falcon trainer's hands
An uneasy passage

ARABIC EVERYTHING

………..

SCHOOL FOR CONVERSIONS

The plain door of your

childhood

like a thin volume of

rosemary

or your palm

the color of cardboard

O, Table for Weary Elbows!

That awful document
of limestone

This sack of olives for the press

The Moors

        make me

Yours—*Langston Hughes*

I am counting knots to distract death.

Historia de la lengua española: A Ghazal

War gives us words and its traffic more words.
All words, a seizing and levy of goods.

Singing waterways, a gardened governance.
Europe eyeing darkly from dense woods.

Loosening parchment with a bit of spit.
What's lost becomes a whorl in the heard.

My body, a watchtower, my arrows within reach.
The figure moves closer and may be my own.

So much of what we say to the future is Arabic.
Ojalá marches forward, through borders and blood.

Fushigi na Chicharrón
for Sergio Mondragón

1.

The body's hidden face
removed of its excesses
is cooked into a codex
that reads:
this little piggy went to market
this little piggy piled high
illuminates
what's meant by surface.

Everywhere a nation awaits,
a cardboard raft
soaks through. Everywhere is
a drink of water
swimming with the dead:

Leagues that can't be reached
or spoken.

2.

A man in the plaza
sweats beneath
the synthetic hide
of historical sacrifice
and does a dance
making tourists
in t-shirts
feel
so alive.

Far north
an altar will be built
for the seamstress
forgotten in piecing
such garments.

3.

The question, as we sit
by the grill, becomes:
What is the real animal
between us?

What skin do we stretch,
scrape and tension with
our desire
for expansion? For books
that leap like bodies
not our own?

So we can never end
with more or less
than this: What
does it mean to start here,
with a *taco de chicharrón*,
as if to say "fushigi na en"
the encounter and consumption of skin
launches every ship?

Without the Ties of
Realistic Representation

*...the model's intrinsic value is that it compensates for the
giving up of actual dimensions with the acquisition of
comprehensible dimensions.*
—Claude Lévi-Strauss, *La Pensée Sauvage*

A helm, a sea
of surrogate
material. The curve
of discovery
factored in
& the ship,
tilted this way & that
against your incompetent
signal. I always make it
to your country
in my structural
mock-up.

Sea Body

I'm beginning to alter the location of this harbor
—Bernadette Mayer

This compass.   This faulty wiring.

This needle trembling north.   This is what lost looks like.

This is <u>way</u> south of progress.

This is experiment, a dangerous
ride, a belly of rocks to pelt late summer.

This dark salt shipwreck.

My, my! Aren't you a ruthless captain!

This is you netting bright fish.

This is the lust of unsentimental waters.

This is a bottomless constellation of bones, dog's juicy memory.

Stretching this home.

Stretching this home.

What Processions

1.

Yes, the fineness of the dead father,
what he couldn't say in life
we'll tell it in wood.

And a surplus of chilled
flowers, the girly grim
of them. (Only the newly heeled
request donations for
the thing that killed them.)

Still, it's not like winning
the centerpiece
of pink carnations
at a bridal shower
or mastering in shop
an arrangement
of baby's breath.

2.

A strip of revved up cars
that never go. A church entrance
: an ice moat
to teach us—really—
about the ever-lasting.

What parades winters are
when they end with a fallen float,

a big white glove
wavering over a crowd.

But why now cringe at the ill-fitted meeting
of microphones and names?

Or demand that clergy
be above Reeboks?

Having tread the aisle well
in both directions, we deliver
our lines genuinely, costumes
fresh from other run-thrus.

3.

Mourning has the crossing guard
in the heat
of summer school.

Six months, and traffic
barely inches
towards him
or away.

O, Flirtatious engine.
O, Demure off-ramp.

My father would see
this midweek wedding

at a country club
as the marriage of lisp
to lockjaw.

But claim the prospect of shrimp
and mango skewers
worth a push
through the bottleneck.

And he'd leave nothing
to chance. A lean in to the DJ
and everyone's
on the dance floor.

Patriotic Song

In the bird's belly a pacifier, a ring, a store
of plastic pellets from which come
toy soldiers and bendable things. The bird
thinks little of the seas that carried
our uncles, or the sudden onslaught
of salmon on our plates. A school
of absence makes vaporous our aims. The symbolic
meal for the immigrant is loaded
with things that swim or fly. There are food riots
in Sierra Leone, Cambodia, Egypt,
Haiti. The bird was found swollen
"by the shores of Tripoli."

*

Some Maritime Disasters This Century

*Do you retain a positive attitude toward maritime service? Are you
looking for dignity or resolution?*

British insurance actuaries have placed sex
as the least reliable form of transportation—
it is estimated that capsizing is a kind
of intimacy. And drowning, a flat contradiction to either.

Why did you spin from island to island?

Even a nugget of earth seemed a large price to pay
for salvation. I would not have been able to use my legs
as salt dervishes. I've come to know the heart
is secretly an archipelago.

Were you conversant in morse code or delirium?

My mouth remains dry, but days before being expelled,
news reports announced a rabid pitbull
guarding an abandoned baby. My ovaries were tested
for patience. Biding results, I took a trip.

Are you familiar with transmitting systems, i.e. a flare for mishaps?

The search for causes, scapegoats, what have you,
is in full flood. But I'm well-versed
in the language of telephones: how to break
a date, how to quell disasters.

*The ferry was nothing less than a series of failed locks. What could
compare in its faulty construction?*

Every so often, let's say a full lunar cycle,
the fundamental concepts of elementary navigation
become unhinged. Mayday mayday is an affair
worth pursuing, as is the mess of lost power.

Waterfront

1.

Dear cartographer,
lasso me some perspective—
I've been robbed
of harbor,
and I got ships coming in.

2.

Where in the world
does a map
document the coordinates
of us on our backs,
in separate rooms,
committing labor
no one discusses,
slaving over a milk-warm heap
of deflection
night after night.

3.

To the taxonomy
of your evasion, darling
I am indentured.

Migration

In sleep, two unlikely
countries bordering.

Bodies vigilant
to attack: at times

Axis, at times
Ally. Tonight we

lie awake, one hand
on each other's

gate. How far
to open it, how far

to slip through.
What casualty

will this bed
bring. Our chests idle

their tired patrol.
In confusion

we might smuggle
each other

past all regret.
And we are only

one foot into the other's
long walk home.

Which direction
to take:

forward or forfeit?

Monogamy
for JS

to crave dismemberment
in a crowd
or to piece together
ghosts
and fuck
their little see-through
parts

(Entropy)

holding yourself
to sleep
your arms pass
through your chest and into
Ohio, then
Boston

This Way of Talking

We have this way of talking, and we have
another. Apart from what we wish and what
we fear may happen.
          —Rumi

What can call itself
language tonight?

You voice hands
over knees

and beg
vacancy,

your body
folded as much

inward
as outward

weaves its
need—

an awkward
signage

wasted

on the
routinely

blind.

What?
A "house"?

My focus
distills

something
akin to "harm"

or, why not,
"hell"

but considering
the hour's

warp

you might
stay for a while

"here"

instead.

Psalms for Happy Hour
for LP

We toast to the tug
becoming a sway

and an admission
waves silently

bye   bye

....

Why read me
the amateur magician's

kit, when instructions
demand dexterity? Love,

my hands tonight are slighted—

Monogamy 2

No two men who wear the same hat
are the same man. Still,
the swirl

of water in the rim
is the circularity of thoughts
on death. He tips his hat

into the street
and so it goes,
this accumulation.

We walk
only so far
into the neighborhood,

rain makes discerning
dangerous.

Framed

The language
of pictures

if we are to
read them

as text
make light

of years
or money spent

in Prague
or health

wasted
in Paterson

so who
we marry

can only
be understood

as we interpret
a good deal

the photographer's
motives,

the dress's
trail

getting caught
in the limo

door. But,
I'd hate to

contemplate it
further

than this page.
Let's have

your students
read the

import
of these visual

cues, affective
advertisements

for making
a run for it

for selling the baby.

Class

It's not work
just because
you can get it.

It's the luck
of the hem
and the heel

a perfectly turned
drinking clause
made readable.

What some call
internal dialogue
my dad would have called

brandy.
It's not work
if you can spell

it. A union line
hemmed against
cold weather

gives Poles
and Spaniards
little to talk about:

pre-printed placards
struggle to rhyme
equality with anything

And Jersey
keeps me rubbernecking
like free verse

can cure
some poor fuck's
lung cancer.

Today, students
are working out
class schedules

and I propose a course
objective of carrying
paint drums

across the length
of my office
until someone gives.

Property

as air becomes small in our diction. We allow little space to fill this or that of the storytelling. Pressed against each other, we are in easy reach of all that completes us. I daydream of bolting past grievances to the ceiling. You write checks in proportion to silence. I remain grounded as we talk—do not gesticulate or mimic (from the Latin root). We pillar up to nothing and our collective history includes not much more than a bed and sometimes a bonfire beneath it. Curtains, a comforter, a name that appears as the infidel in the play. A cat and a knife. Either could have been retractable, we assume. Such is progress a tepid concession, a heated pad against the neck. To soothe this appetite for what old estates afford. Slow to the drawl, I quickly fire the bride announcing appliances. If we were far away, if you were truly Asian or a tug boat in a black and white film, a short story could be easily laid out, but the neighborhood shrinks like a favorite dress. I want to know how everything changes with the price of admission. As I hold this balsamic, I catch a glimpse of myself and realize

I fit only in the way you press your bed into corners to make room for early morning dancing. Of late, your feet perform no more than the usual movements from kitchenette to phone, but there are matters of spontaneity that cannot be ignored—you may require instantly a plié and an effortless jump. My unwashed clothes demand a center, not a side or indiscreet mound, right dead, my panties forming an impudent pink eye. Enough to walk around. Never imagined sedition could simply mean well-placed laundry. And while you struggle through Chinese lessons, I am dark hair clogging the matter you've been revising in the shower; a certain something to be fine-tuned before announcing. Meanwhile, I practice a flame-retardant thing, a thing sealed with hardy plastic, a buckled thing. There's no script for this unfolding act. We hold it in, trying to materialize the off-planet where you are the short guy at the party and I'm the tiger without conscience. To say a phrase like my feet could never determine the price of marble is to turn it up loud.

The New Nude

He feels deep in his armpits
the cross-hairs of purpose, the dalliances
of the body
the splayed goat
condemns.

And what is the old desire
if not blood
smeared on a woman's
chest? How are our mothers
not like this meat?

The boy in the museum
holds his father's
hand. They exit one room
and find themselves projected
in another.

"This is no last supper, and the ironic friendship
which brings us together consists in knowing this,
while peering with a 'squinty eye' toward this
cannibalism in mourning"

We sin
in the safety

of burning
houses

our bodies
in mute
emergency

demanding
pageantry

amid
collapse

...

a heated
confession

changes

the room's
shape.